Stepping Over Imaginary Lines

Stepping Over Imaginary Lines

Nicholas Lee Wasmer

Lemon Pie Publishers
8 Golf Road
Springfield, IL 62704

Stepping Over Imaginary Lines. Copyright 1996 by Nicholas Lee Wasmer. Printed and bound in the United States. All rights reserved. No part of this book may be printed, reproduced or stored in any medium, without written permission from the publisher, except by a reviewer, who may quote brief passages in a review. Published by Lemon Pie Publishers, 8 Golf Road, Springfield, Illinois 62704. Limited edition.

ISBN 0-9650879-0-5

Cover Design by Michael D. Wasmer

Printed on recycled paper

Attention colleges, professional organizations and fund raisers: Quantity discounts are available on bulk purchases for training, fundraising or gift giving. Special posters, booklets or custom work are available to fit your specific requirements. For additional information, contact the Marketing Department of Lemon Pie Publishers.

*My only job is to be pure
the rest comes naturally.*

Heart Line	1
Personal Power	2
As It Unfolds	4
Two Doors	5
It's Your Movie	6
Cartoon Land	7
Trying Is Not a Good Word I Am Told	8
This Old Life	9
On a Hill of Red	10
Katrina	11
And Who Must Answer Any Question?	12
Starvation	13
Desire at First Glance	16
Sit Down Pay Attention	18
Delicious Light Love!	19
Set Me Free	20
Whirling Vibes	24
Inner Treasure Cookin' While I'm Lookin'	26
On a Jelly Roll	28
Looking at the Scene	30
Togo ala gogo	33
Carry Me to that Sanctuary	34
THE JESTER	36
What Ever Happened to that Clean Forest Buzz?	38
Just a Step	39
Monkey Suit	40
Big Play Spasm	41
Soak It In	42
Fluids and Flow	44
I Know What A Tribulation Is	45
Standing in a Puddle	46
Fishen' 4 Real Again	48
Abandon Ship!	50
Walking Through Ashes of the Past	51
Possibly Revealing	52

Armageddon Is Coming	53
Pure + Natural	54
Whom Shall I Fear	55
At A Rabbits Pace	55
AND THIS	63
On the Train	67
Simple 1	68
Simple 2	69
Tune Jazz	70
The Choice of Our Head	72
Blow Your Mind Automation	74
It Is Or It Isn't	76
The Sanctuary Cutter	78
Emotional Propaganda	79
My Will Doesn't Own	80
This is the Nineties...	82
Out Side	83
Rerunning Frantically	84
Where We Have Been	86
Visionary	88
Heart and Soul	89
An Essay on What Needs to be Said	90
Butterflies and Bees	91
I Want to Break Society's Toys	92
Defunkatizer	93
In the Fog, No, Out of It	94
Twisted Wire	95
Soul Less	96
Picketing and Protesting	97
Politics	98
When You Got Love	99
Return of the Undone	100
Corn on the Cob	101
Your Message	102

People will always test you
If you want to pass those tests
Speak of your truths.

Heart Line

I think I have too much on my mind
    this time
that's a dead line
a live line is something
    you can roll from
to the next
    insight on paper
but that is out of line
    and this is in rhyme
see this poem
    was dead from beginning
bunk line after
    bunk line
to meet a dead line
    on time
what can you get from a bunk line
    taking up space without grace
just to take up space
    and make you bored
wasting your time and mine
let's make every line have the
most individually momentous purposeful
    message it can
this world is one large poem
and everyone of us has a heart line
    thumping here in this space
    at this time

Personal Power

Take a look into yourself to see
who you are and who you'll be
When the levels get huge
are you getting smaller?
are you only short because
      someone is taller
on this down fall
      going up
I feel down on this and that
I want a movement
not the analyzation of one
      beaming some light into the sun
what time is right?
what time is wrong?
I know how to sing
      I know my own song
tell me when it counts
and tell me not to chicken out
my fear is just a shadow
and so it's due to the unknown
until I can see/it's true form is unshown
      Personal Power
the power of love
      pushing me higher
to what lies above
while something in me still disagrees
this place right here seems safer to me
to some degree
this moment, this state
I'd say it's satisfactory
      simply
in tune
      with the room
After the afternoon
      yet ain't there anything to say

I want to care
        I want to care
but sometimes the feeling
        just isn't there
And then it jumps up on the couch
        to sit and love
        and remove those doubts
of my own head bouts
See her eyes
        see you
Where the spirits reside
in their own world's mind
        to learn what they have yet to learn
        to see God

As It Unfolds

As it unfolds...
    in all degrees of realities
where, why and how
as it unfolds
    slower which is good and bad
I feel like a see-saw
    putting together a jigsaw
    puzzled by the lockjaw
    science of silent pa
    talking through clairvoyant law
    eating the truth barehanded and raw
as it unfolds
    core center climax
or is it now unfolding?
    or is that past tense?
How long has it been since?
    delectrocuting the fence
take off that filter and dance
to see God in every glance
as it unfolds
    like lifting your arms off your gut
    no need to ask what
your intuition tool is no fool
open your eyes, ears, nose, mind and heart
    to pull life into
    to pull love into
        Here
    into now
    into it, Shine!

Two Doors

So, you are stuck with this
unmakable decision
does karma exist?
do you believe in paying for your actions
and getting paid for your actions
you don't want shame
don't purchase it
You want love --- give it.
brotherly love --- sisterly love
do you think God is love?
to love the world let it flow through you
and it will be in you
how? I'd say it's in your perception
want to change your environment
change your head
I know it is not easy sometimes
and when you think you're in the clear
and moving up it's easy to fall
if God is love and love is loving
you are always loved...
surrender to it
trust that your decisions
all may lead you for the best
let time reveal it all.

It's Your Movie

Doesn't anyone want
someone to know them
to shine self into the sun
More than anything
I want to find someone to know
but, I don't know who.
it's like a movie
interactive
how well do you understand
the actors?
play your part by
following your heart
the movie can be classic
a magnificent piece of art
life's story of your mind
life's story doesn't rewind
scene by scene
unfolding a message
a play of the senses
knowing is a weird thing
feeling, seeing, and being
just know the moment
with reserved judgment
trust yourself
you are justified and still alive
gotta be doing something
Right!

Cartoon Land

You know
looking through the digital window
cartoon land is at hand.
Striking like a balloon powered
steam engine
breaking through the thick
cloud of ingenuous deception
like a thing straight out of imagination
I'm gonna build me a space ship
to fly my mind
back home
dreams are launching pads
just spread your wings
AND FLY
Realing through the air
Have you paid your fare?
The ticket maestro
won't let you go
If you don't care.
Hop on that souped up purple tricycle and ride
off into the pure styled sun.
To be one
Smiling Dream State
rolling on green hills
Hair blowing in the wind
while it speaks to unchain our minds
to groove along with the flow
the true way for to go
Swirling it all back into
the fantasticle deep blue.
We are sailing on the river on a
mobius trip steam engine cycle.
rainbow styled
no body over bored
in and out of traveling mechanisms
like the chocolate factory
voyaging in a cup of tea

Trying Is Not a Good Word I Am Told

Trying is not a good word
I am told
I'm trying to be good
to forgive
and to live
but I don't feel like I should
I have got pain
and it only adds to my pain
to know that it's not real
that it's something I can heal
my ribs make it hard to breathe
and my brains make it hard to be
I am told that when I get my lesson
I will be healed
and my joy will be real
something I can feel
Is there a moral obligation I've failed to fulfill?
their book, the knowledge of good and evil
it's the apple from the garden
and its interpretation switches
as they try to understand
enforcing false rules on man
this is the knowledge you failed to earn yourself
cherish your misunderstood twisted wealth
they fell for power in an hour
and in a similar wagon I am trying to understand
that which takes much time to comprehend
when should I indulge in the feelings
when should I conflict?
it's a fit I cannot though
then I don't really know
but the warrior knows without knowing
am I coming or going
like the sun
do I have my own
      empty pockets
      full heart
or the other way around?

This Old Life

This old life
of struggle and strife
do the pleasures outnumber the pains?
what do I have to lose, what do I have to gain?
knockin' on doors
don't always know what to look for
inner tormentation
      I roll out of bed
gotta pick my head up off the floor and roll
      like a stone
no big deal, but what is?
It's all a bout of opposition
which side are you on
      choose a position
or I will for you.
Yet who comforts a weary soul,
tells me what I need to know,
Who loves? where is that warm cup of coffee
and forgivable cigarette waiting for me?
who is going to step down into my mind
and cut the roots in my wine cellar?
Keep knocking on the door
      I gotta get thru
Now I get frustrated
      it ain't no good
Let's find the right
      state of mind.
So let go cause I ain't got nothing to lose,
 grab hold of a silver,
no brass, doorknob
      could even be gold
Wouldn't matter
      simple twist of fate
ask me how I feel and open up the gate
no longer knocking on heaven's door...
      What's it for?

. a hill of red
 .d a guitar play a man
 .ght in the song of worry
 .ig of might, an epic story.

 .ne other side of the hill
 .oneliness talks to a maiden
many wonder whys with no attempts to answer
 there flies a hawk solitude looses a feather.

though nothing lost nothing is gained
 and sit do the alone, sun, snow and rain
no bottle with a note no carrier pigeon around
 no desire to cover any unknown ground.

Comes day comes night slipping by
 both heads tilted right with eyes looking up
and the same music plays slipping eyes
 close and dream in seas of chance and hope.

Gradually they awake to walk picking flowers
 up the red hill from both sides to look up to see
to think who is that looking at me in winds a drift
 they glide to feel God in a touch a lift in deed.

Were we to ever see the other side of the red hill
 silently awaiting you for me why did we wallow
with loneliness as company should we chance if we will
 step on up to the top of the hill of red.

Katrina

Fortune lies inside a crooked oak tree
winter days and winds speak to me
a whisper as the first snow flake comes gradually
to full fledged music drifting here over seas

time negotiates with interpersonal space
to bring us both into this place
frozen in loves eternal embrace
how sweet the smell how sweet the taste

you held me and diluted my air
how would I disagree with one so fair
who showed me a flower more divine than life
mesmerized in a glow a tide of the universal flow

If I dove into you as a dolphin to the sea
would you also receive me so gracefully?
Were I to see you now, were I to see you
asleep to kiss a cheek so soft and true

Were I to tell, I love you...

And Who Must Answer Any Question?

And I learn my lessons
for my willingness to see
due to my curiosity
doubting now,
all which I knew
   to be true
looking for a light
   to shine
   through
This is me
at this time
in this realm
of eternity
forever present
in the now
where I am
and where I've been
and where ever I'll be
   in the end
I feel I can make it
   somehow
I must look to see
if I've been right
has truth drifted from
   my sight
am I coming closer to
   that which I seek?
is it making me strong?
is it making me weak?
what lies ahead for me to
fight?
as monsters are
only monsters to me
I could be the enemy.
   Fighting anything
may be like kicking
   dandelions
only spreading the seeds
creating more weeds
is that why they tell me
   to let it be...
speaking words of wisdom
   providing keys
doing onto others
   as I would
have them do to me
so I will bring gifts to
the squirrels
   and to the ducks
   and to the fish
swimming in the muck
hoping to lighten not
   only their load
but also their road
if I wish
   to really see
I must sacrifice
some old beliefs
and look again in
   tranquility
for that golden dust
   on the moth's back
to provide me with
the knowledge I lack.

Starvation

Starvation
when I should have crops
and the rain pours down
but the rain,
      the sun will mop,
Until then may I drown.
now time passes me by a lot
time and food are now commodities
it's one for thirty
      and little do I learn
All this time and what do I earn?
One cup of coffee in the morning
      rots in the belly
      and I have no flow
      to ease the blow.
What is happening to the life worth living?
A priest would say that I am sinning
      and a speech
      destroys the peace
and the woods will I never reach?
Where art the times when food was free,
      and from a friend
      was a bite to eat?
I sit in the front seat
      but I can't drive...
It should all revolve around knowledge
      and in pursuit of peace
      life should be a college
      and everyone should teach.
The environment is a textbook
      I hope you take a look
      to interpret its reasons
      and it's rhymes.
I don't beg you, for I know you have the time.
The park should be the town square
      and wisdom you shall find there
      but now we just stare

at the teachers in the front of the room
or attempt to sleep amongst the gloom.
I cannot speak, just face the front
while my belly burns without a meal.
I have no money and too many
    morals to steal...
for sit do I in the echo chamber
and ignore my body and my mind
I don't want to drag them down
    with so much of my time.
When have people grown their fear?
When have people forgotten to hear?
I am not standing in the clear
    and these are not the woods.
These are not the woods,
    this is only a tree
    in the woods,
    which is famished.
Will there be a day
    when this final tree dies?
Shall all ignorant lies be banished
    and everyone understand the truth
    how it works...
for when you know how it works
    easily
    you may follow the changes.
because nature does not follow yours.
Let nature play lead guitar
    and all of life
    follow its rhythm...
for as the spider follows it's web
    in the breeze
we may follow nature
    with ease.

We learn from mistakes
      we evolve from death
let evolution carry its breath
we need not better transportation
      for everywhere you may find
        your vacation.
Let everyone step back and breathe
especially the ones who started the feed.
I ask you to heed and stop
      for if you look up
      you are at the top
just banging your head trying to climb.
Buy a house and build a garden
you may live there without a burden
you need not wear your shoes upon your grounds
see the beauty all around...
for you have made a life of pleasure
in this you discover the real treasure.
Others "success" in society is faulty
but you have grown your own parsley.
      And I sit
      in the echo chamber
      much more
will someone hear these words I adore?
      I wonder,
        should I write more...
Most people are too caught up anymore
I'm sick of mislead people who will not listen,
when a wise man speaks you hear them hissing.
But into the woods will I walk
      for my troubles, it seems,
        I cannot caulk
Into the woods I walk till the end
for a country of starvation
      I cannot defend!

Desire at First Glance

Broke in two　　　　　the jewelry shop　　　fanciful in appearance
I walk with who　　　 and casually stop　　　desire at first glance
look on through　　　 its covered top　　　　see its colored dance
who speaks of usefulness and what we really need?
Eyes caught in glance at first desire made them heed
fragility uselessness diamonds watches jewelry
　　　　EVERYTHING MUST BE SOLD!
I want it to　　　　　the fashion top　　　　furs forget to dance
very common attitude　it must stop　　　　　take an inner glance
look on through　　　 the Babylon shop　　　it's the devil's dance
　　　of desire and appearance
emptiness is no sort of virtue reaching out just won't do
　　　　forget your cover and tell me was that really you?
Self indulgence is not a human attitude
　　　　it's the quest of the animal and the flesh
　　　　it's the anger and jealousy the devil likes best
can you love?　　　　can you be free?
　　　　When you look at a diamond what do you really see?

Sit Down Pay Attention

Go to school
        sit down pay attention
Listen for your lessons
        I"m talking about
                HIGH SCHOOL
Not the place falsely termed high school
        where the teachers are programmed
                to program you
                to be as everyone else
Never concentrating on variety
the best variety is the intellectual type
who don't subscribe to the government's hype
who are all looking from different
        perspectives
        for the same thing
all looking for the truth
        why
it will set them free
while false school restricts you
Go to High school
I'm talking high vibrations
        real revelations
Peace

Delicious Light Love!

Should I not worry
about where I am flowing
indirection
to my erection
above my old self
to rest with the
fairies and the elf
at times I wish
I were a tree
so as not to worry
about my intentions
or my addictions
moving to love
if I may
to rise above
      the clouds today
      pink and gray
stand strong
I can tell my brother.
Sometimes I wish
he would tell me
or is that the job of my
mother

I'm alive
I'm ALIVE
smile and let me live
I still have love to give
I have worried before
I shall worry more
but I do have
my times of peace
Proud land
      proud land
I shall find you if I can
at the good time theater
rear view mirror
      shall it be there?
I want simple,
      always have
but still I don't know
where to go
break through sun
      SHINE
Break through
right on time
to ease my mind

Set Me Free

I was driving behind
a Mercedes Benz
when we passed the officer.
Speeding with a wave and a smile
went the rich to continue his miles
but, for me the lights went on
and I was stopped to wait a while.
Troubles already to my name,
I was who the officer came to blame.
A violation of safety assigned to my name.

One for speaking out,
one for taking out
the air of "decency" they feel was about.
From this harsh reality,
I want to escape
and they feel I deserve
      A Black Cape
      A Doper
when those Alabama cops
never seem sober.
They say cast all those into the jail void
      Hide them from me and my boy
Avoid the Noid!
Writers and great thinkers,
politicians and drinkers
I guess we all have a story to tell.
When the true light gets shown
Who will still feel well?
And smile, still taking the pain,
from those thoughts which
misplace the blame.
Jumping to conclusions
creates some warped illusions,
but who is to say,
who to believe
but yourself.

Put another misunderstanding
    on the shelf.
Take away my doubts
    Let me know what this is really about!
I'm scared of my own traps
    of mental anguish
Being read into this theme
    of death
I want to escape to catch my breath.
The more I think I know
the farther down it seems I may go.
When I can't see, hear, or feel
    what I know is there...
What is real?
Why should I care?
Sharing this thought
    brings blank stares
Making me wonder who is there.
But people are like birds
    whom easily scare
who fail to see what I know exists.
A ship of fools
with their useless tools
all being guided by the insane rules
and going through the meat grinding schools
to support the greed that
    breaks us all
which is protected by
a wall of cannonballs.
Someday something will fall
let us make sure that it's the wall
so we may have the best government
which is none at all.
When we get up and stand up
let us stand tall
hear that call for Freedom
    Let it Ring
and let it keep ringing.

This is Truth
think what you think
and be as you will
there is no one to hurt
without making yourself ill.
When you get down to how you really feel
    are you missing something?

Can you hear the ring?
Could you see this thing?
I'm talking love with life
leaving behind the cold
ignorance is getting old.
I want to talk to people
who know how to speak
whose words are strong
not half-witted and weak.
Still seeking truth
with more than everyday proof.
The rich may get by with a cheap smile
for a while
but, the cop let me off.
And down the road a couple of miles
    that rich car added a hefty dent
    to it's style
He was on the car phone all alone...

Whirling Vibes

We feed it all back around
no extraneous speaking
it all means something
if you look at it right
life's little instructions
discovered by the means
      of symbolism
Can't you see..
it's not a matter
      of good eyesight
it's a matter of insight
in this matter
      of fact
it may all be seen
depending on where you
      begin
      to gleam
think my words as I think
      out loud
when the words don't come out
      no one will hear
when the words come out
      the listening is in
      more than the ear
you may fail to accept
      if the moron rejects
everyone's vision is altered
      by everyone else
for many times in our entangled
      corruptions and misunderstandings
the truth is so simple it's ignored
and the fallacies so obvious they
      are taught
that's all drama
warranted by life
and it puzzles me so
      I don't feel like
      letting go

The drama... The drama
    you know
do we require it
    does it inspire you?
I want an altered point of view...
but you don't worry
    don't get angry
that would only make
    you seem
to be mean
as one man thinks a thought
some of it gets absorbed by
the consciousness cloud
the more people he spreads it to
the more people thinking the thought
the more of the thought gets absorbed into
    the consciousness cloud
and every once in a while
    lightning strikes
I have a thought
    tonight
    thinking of love.

Inner Treasure Cookin' While I'm Lookin'

When I can use love
    When I choose love
even the stars smile on me
    from above
and they can see the soul
Live today I heard Hendrix say
well all right, ok
I can dig that
pop a brilliant thought
into my magic hat
Speak proud
    Speak loud
Nothing but existing
Woo Wee that can be
    for me
Through the fog
    is that
    surrounding me
    if that's what I see
Who do you listen to?
    self, inner self, outer self
    more real?
        for real?
What do you feel?
What's that magic
Yours? Yours?
Who is it for?
You claim that divinely

Manifesting destiny
did you make it yourself
    naturally hee hee
Or is that just what you want to believe?
do you figure it's impossible to conceive
    giving up
just to work on filling your cup
people who believe in God
Want something to look up to

and they say if you sin he will forgive you
    that sounds true
the problem with that
what is the problem with that?
is it out of humility that it's God I see
    feel and breathe occasionally?
I really don't feel it's just me
although most experience it differently
it's the same thing
    that gives us our wings
    and makes us really sing.

On a Jelly Roll

Kansas City looked
    broken down
48 murders the sign said
could there be too many guns around?
We can pass on through
    with my little sticker
    helping us get there quicker
it says one word
that needs to be heard
road, road be clear and
    straight to our abode
left lane time
moving into a one way line
    from the east
going with <u>love</u> in this
    mechanical beast
What was he trying to say
    to help me on my way
don't just listen to yourself
copy others for great wealth
I wouldn't do that
    but I do listen
to see the truth glisten
what about my inner guide
    isn't it the same that's inside
    all people far and wide
the same which spoke to Socrates,
    Plato or any of these
    great thinkers
    thought makers
What it comes down to
    clear and simple
What comes down to
    clear and simple?
is the power of love
that which none may rise above
here is to your health
and your power to love, to feel

soul on a roll
this is sacred land
    learn to admire
even the freeway has a speed limit
    Everything free has a rule in it
Topeka, Eureka
    looks enlightening
but even that can be frightening
    energy comes from lightning
and thunder never put no one under
    catch me, catch me
that other fish said we were falling
but that real fish is always calling
    he loves us
    he loves us all
don't put his love behind a wall
    chance, chance
community chest
before you take a test
    get a good rest
everyday is a test
    just do your best
Wanamaker
    shake your moneymaker
machine man
    or free-willed land
don't be a castle made of sand
when we get to Junction City
things will sure be pretty
cause they have room for us
    and our magical rolling bus
making it there through confusion or clear
keeping Kansas clean
    a sea of green
people with as much color as the environment
    plain and simple
doing fine
    walking in line

Looking at the Scene

Looking at the scene
In the station to hit home
Relieve me of those
      looks unknowing what to say
that make me look around
      not knowing my way
when I don't know what I'm doing
I'm being self conscious
who to look at
don't want them to think
      I'm looking for a wink
don't want them to feel pressured
I don't want to feel pressured
don't want to stare
I display my confusion
looking around, then looking away
To the void which lays
      in my mind.
Why do I trudge through the things
everybody seems to know?
I seem to feel the rain
      to roll around in the snow.
Don't know where I going
      I'm never too sure
putting my hand over my eyes
      is not the best cure
Flew into the store
through the door
like the trolley to make believe
I don't know what for
though I like reasoning adventures
when it comes to the big pictures
you can't buy treats just by the name
so you hire a psychic to let you
know of the chocolate goo
in the silver wrapper attire
but that did not work, my friend
      as vanilla cream was in store

My train is arriving
    the people, getting up
to go out in the hot sun oh, what fun
With a little sole on my shoe
when you got soul
anything's possible
    Right Jimi?
I look up to see
someone look at me
No reason
    just bored I guess
as we transgress on down the road
You make a language and
    the Lord will speak to you through it
    you give them meaning
and that's what you can lean on
and on and on
I see you grandpa, sir
your hat tipped like a gangster
we are all in the same boat
we got to keep it afloat
don't go waving your gat
that's not where it is at
Why do I still judge some people
    When I know in my heart we can be equal
look at what we have in common
    that we can work on together
help me escape the talking trap of
    complaining about the weather
let my words flow with the grace of a feather
    I said something
    because my train is late
that I missed it this morning
    it was on time
    something I'm not used to
ain't that great
    and those words being the last said
are the ones that keep bouncing around in

      my head
but that is all right cause it's ok
      and I'm northbound momma
riding in aisle seat
this is really neat
writing what comes to mind
so I can see what I may find
      out
      about
out and about
with and without
I know what I know
I go where I go
if someone is reading
I'll continue writing until
I talk. He hit the bar
      right on time
I should have asked what she
      was reading to ease
the quiet that is to come
parts of me walking around
does any of this hit home
      or does it all
does it make you want to stand tall
      stall or
                                        fall?
I ask you to stand, my brothers.

Togo ala gogo

Good joke, way to gogo on my togo to night, hey gallop with me on the scene, jump back five individual spaces, too used to having the joy button to change, that didn't do a thing, hand it over and move to the toll to pay for the road you just walked down. Not like you really wanted to accelerate into this funk e toll bar, the most commonly used, but you didn't tell anyone, how would they know. Is this you or what you are thinking? or just jargon of a non existent sage who for the time being exists as far as you don't know he might tomorrow. have never been ignored today, but only listen to those which look like they know... cause everyone else is full of the truth that you don't want to hear. Is there something we should do as opposed to what we shouldn't? they should know that clearly but must miss it truly. You of all people should know all about why people don't wanna listen unless it's just brambling and rambling for half a laugh which leaves you half empty.. a whole hearted laugh stains eternity like a rosy smile on your toes.. who else knows this if anyone does. Like to play with berries in berry ville. If you like berries they can always be found just look at your feet they are all along the ground like to go there and chill up on the hill where all of the buckets spill it really is a thrill every one is merry in berryville. Unless they don't like berries... then they walk on down, just around the bend fruit town may be found, have a banana apple or a pear if you like fruit every thing is there... or vege out in veggie ville where everything is super chill. Dinner at the diner tonight or last chance cafe. lotus let us smell a perfume which out weights the stench... So we are sitting on a bench and may I take your order... well what I want to know is How heavy is the wait... maybe four or five pounds... oh you are a girl, let me help you spend your paper-thin time my knee isn't too good but I can put a handle on the pounds. If you let me come to London with you if I may some day. time well spent ten scents at a time, dime after dime... park closes at dark safety finally fire works on destruction, it can be creative if you see it my way, just started righting some wrongs. Hold it there hold what where? you want me to what... You know what I mean -HUH- take your hands out of your pants you fool ingrid - my grandma- you fool her when you walk on your hands she looks at your feet... yea I saw her in a past life, she had forty thieves like Ali Baba ran Bob and I did though we had nothing worth stealing and even if we did I believe in cosmic justice I mean you can't take from me unless I don't deserve what I got. If I haven't got it paid off.

Carry Me to that Sanctuary

A conscious conversation
      is a great vacation
I must submit to the truth
as I sit here
in a small sea of green
      grass
grass better than
      any car
It's raining but not on my pad
      scratch that
I carried a ladybug to a sanctuary of trees
the thunder is attacking but does not scare me
      is thunder caused by fear
      or the other way around
      like a chicken and an egg
TORNADOES IN HER DREAMS
      What could it mean?
I like to be alone
      sometimes
but not to be an island.
      I like to do weird things
      to see what they bring
I like to come prepared
      but don't always know what I need
don't want mosquito bites
but I could die from repellent
What makes these bugs
      hang around me?
how can you be so smart but miss the easy part?
how can you be so good but not know what you should?
I've pondered that
but don't really care
Bench looks good
      but I want to walk on
I said be loving now forever
      wrote it up
And stuck it to the billboard
Walked into a coffee shop
thought I'd get a coffee

      Sweet sinsations
      talk talk talk
I'd rather take my dog on a walk
         but it's all good they say
           It could be but for the moment
I'm not sure it is
      is that bad
or would that being bad prove my point
        I'd rather have ice cream
but you know what they
say bout the grass being green
at least someone gives me
        an honest smile
          the hello of the soul
Not the fastest not the quickest
but going slow can be
        delicious
give a man a fish, he'll eat for a day
teach a man to fish, he'll live forever
the sign for Jesus is a fish
Am I getting too religious
         about a coincidence?

THE JESTER

"Take me away" said the Jester
to a land where nothing ends
I'm tired of starting and stopping
to a land where I begin
this land I will visit
only grows and grows but never ends
I've changed my mind
take me away to another land
Where people are loving
and people hold hands
We hug and laugh and have lots of fun
and there is no telling when we'll be done
the king raised his arm...
as rainbows of darkness show across the sky
I close my eyes and began to fly
the world became small eensy-teensy
meaning nothing
as it always has
a black hole it became
And I, with my requests
just floated out in space
until I found another planet
that was purple with pink stripes
I swam and swam looking at it
hoping I'd get there tonight
I then arrived on a planet anew
the jester yelled out to the moon
take me away to a land of flowers
strawberry fields covering the dunes
So, there was silence as the moon
closed it's eyes and you felt the powers
shifting, changing, flipping around
I then found myself...
engaging
in an amazing trance hooked up with a
goddess in eyes to eyes combat
an attack by the jester grabbed her lips
and held them there as time became no concept
and life became a possession of no importance

so we began to dance...
We danced for hours and hours,
as time is an illusion
and the kiss finally ended.
And again we look into each
other's eyes.
But I the jester got lost
lost in a time warp continuum
Whatever that may be
then sacrificing my innocence
I made love to the goddess.
She took me away
away from life
into Death
the land everyone will explore.
Some might hate it, others adore,
light but dark, sticky while smooth.
Chaos
things constantly changing
as in life
but with a stronger effect.
No one has control over any one thing.
No one.
My mind caught me mid-way drinking a cup of coffee
laced like a pair of LA Gears with Lucy
and the fan blade seemed still
yet it was fluctuating, oh yes, it was!
Yet I could not take it, opportunity, there yet,
I could not take,
So the devil
became upset and brought me home once again
to talk with the Jester.
Who was I.
Who was I?
Into the clouds we shot,
then over, over the clouds
or maybe just the end.

What Ever Happened to that Clean Forest Buzz?

Some times you want
to grab the greed by its....neck
and hang it
if you don't apply the good values
when they count
it doesn't count
We can be happy without all that
all that takes our time
for luxury
and deceives our minds
from truth
and philosophy
I can see the trees screaming
with all of their beauty
for a better world
until every man accepts their beauty
they will be cut, like our breath
could it be a test or a hero's quest
would they say not to mind it
cause they know if you look
there you might find it...
and they are scared you may
see who's behind it.
But we have nothing to lose
'cause if we are right, it's all right
'cause we know where you've been
and, hey man,
deception is out, truth is in.
You better watch out, I ain't lying.
I don't feel we owe anything but love and support to society
set an example of worldly piety
Over the garbage to the end of town
this clean forest buzz
it won't let me down
because I'm rolling on the river

Just a Step

Through the thick all pervading mist rising over the grave yard walk four men carrying a casket. Following the casket are several people dressed in black. It is a funeral and these people are sad. There is a man wearing a crop top and cut off blue jeans telling jokes to lighten up the crowd. His jokes are not working. So he walks off through the mist.

Pilot, still in his crop top, hops an iron spiked fence and leaves the grave yard. He walks down the side walk on Teal Street. He has a smile on his face and walks in an etiquettely advanced pace.

  just a step
  just a step away is death
  from this world
  alternative universe
  alternative vibe
  ready yeah
          yeah ready
  just a step is death
  just a step for this picture to unfold
   to reveal its core
  consciousness shift
  whole picture in store
  just a step is death
  pay off your debts
  matches and cigarettes
  just one more breath
   just one more time
   just one more guess
    just one more climb
    just one more dance
     just one more chance
  if I may, if I might
   have one more try
   to get it right

Monkey Suit

The man in the monkey suit
with the makeup I had furnished
talks in riddlish jukes
topics go undiscussed
spending time with the devil
dancing like they say
who lays it all level to make you go his way
do I let words cut as the truth often can?
you reap what you sew
I know but I don't know
It's my world in a sense
unusualness an odd disease
no need to get tense
yet take it as you please

the man in the monkey suit
      is a reference book on death
leaves you to question the now
      to praise for every breath

can't help but delve my way to the answer untold
conversation regressions to see the truth unfold
is it just a flicker in the night
or something to be known?
hope I live to see the light
am I blind or is it unshown?

wouldn't hate that ride on first impression
as the movie will begin no voice is mindless
to delicately describe the expression
you feel that the music knows you timeless
what I really want to know
is did you listen to the music
preach throughout the show?

Do you listen to the music
and apply it to the flow?

Big Play Spasm

No core of information
      you have to pick and choose
keep in mind unity
      and the burning of the fuse

endorsed by muscle magazine
fresh tasty composite shrimp tale
of Edward Adam's dirty forum
hop on to that wagon team
sweaty flesh of a humpless whale
father and child reunion

how many people swear to God
the distractive alternative to religion
tactful intelligent play books
better than real grass it's sod
information power stations
television's many pronged fish hooks

unlimited jeans universal guarantee
as sheep fall prey to sarcasm
gangs of the same shoes
suitable barbed wire mystery
waiting for the big play spasm
keep on measuring the burning fuse

No core of information
      you have to pick and choose
keep in mind unity
      and the burning of the fuse

Soak It In

It's all in your head
but has it's own rules
rapes from you your time
turns brothers to fools.
Find a path for life
which does not devour,
where we need not move
upon the hour.
Living life from life,
not a TV's depiction
we need not get caught
in all of the fiction.
Reserving judgment
until we know
and employing our love
the only way to go.
Change is constant
as time is constant
and does that make it true?
And what is true?
All we know in any situation
could be useless in another
so readiness in the moment is the key
readiness to learn
keep adding files to our minds
keep adding notes to our finds
keeping open to our times.
The times they are a changing....
Let us not live in vaults
limited by our faults
trust the truth, use your wisdom tooth.
I am a sponge of limitless volume
although its often hard
to get in the corners.
Sitting once more
in my place on the hilltops

you can call out my name
but shouted from any other place
it could not be the same.
Swimming once again in the river
    ever changing
but swimming in any other place
    it could not be the same
Thinking, once more of the world
all that's there, it is all one
I am a piece and the same
I am a piece of coal
    adding my part to the flame

Fluids and Flow

The feel of thought is all there is
    to a human.
And it is to be seen as we walk upon
    and gleam and snarl over the land
    ...that we are out of flow.
We watched the bees collect the pollen during
    the lovely fall.
We wanted privacy and took up space
    and around the place we built a wall.
    ...that wall was out of flow
It was knocked down by the floods
    and 'round the water grew the woods.
We chopped for lumber, dug for oil
    slaughtered the food and would
    if we could, eat the moon.
Plastic is chasing me and I am
    with no where to run
    for plastic isn't fluid
    It's an immortal rejector of the flow.
We were given no trash
    but we now have a mess.
No work needed be done
    we could have solely had fun.
Now We Are On The Run...
    Flowing away from the river...

I Know What A Tribulation Is

I know what a tribulation is
but they can be big deals
I don't know why
that's just how I feel
I've got everything that I
need
    to be happy
right now
and I know how
but when I feel like it
    even if I don't
I can make myself sad
although that feeling
    can be bad
I know what a tribulation is
this is not mine
    nor is it his
and the sun and I are one
and my writings are no less
    writings of the sun
Wallace Stevens wrote that
and we are all part of the sun
not aliens
no matter how much they
can swear
we are one
no matter of time
and no matter where we
may come from or go to
this is me and that is
    you

but I repeat
and don't stop
recording the same thoughts
going over the top
ahhh it's spilling
I guess I'll get a mop
but I'm outside
and I know
    what a tribulation is
this is a mess
but it is not mine
and it is not his
so the mess will stay
and rot and rot
never to clot
unless someone will say
it is my mess
and with the same thought
    it's yours
but I have to say that
even though we are one
that mess belongs to
    the sun
that mess belongs to
    everyone
we'll have to work
    through this tribulation
because until that mess is
cleaned there will be
no vacations!

Standing in a Puddle

I'm standing in a puddle
can't find no way out
raining so hard
      and it keeps growing
ain't no ripples
got to get this water flowing
standing in a puddle
can't find no way out
it's saturating me
and Saturday's waiting
I keep kicking the water
and it still won't stop the clouds
it's raining so hard that I just can't see

and the puddle keeps growing
it's up to my knees
I don't know where to go
I don't know who to see
and this puddle I'm afraid
      is about to drown me

It's telling me ain't no wave gonna reach the clouds
      they get their fun
                                they get their thrills
they don't realize their water spills

I think I'll just have to grow gills
I can make out from all the pain that
      this is no beautiful country rain
        falling on me
        falling on me
        I just can't see
I'm standing in a puddle
lightening strikes
restricted from my inalienable rights
      to life

liberty the idea
    prison the fact
names and names
    in stacks upon stacks
will God remove the clouds to let his light
    dry my puddle
or do I make it worse
    with my tears
it's a state of anticipation
    which creates these fears
I'm a coiled spring
    they don't want tangled in their gears
I just want to talk
    they don't want to hear
so I sit down in the puddle
    and have another beer
ain't nobody gonna open a door
    let me come in and out of the storm
when locks are the norm
and if I stretch too high
    lightning may strike and those defend me
    would say take a hike
standing in a puddle
    with a tear on my face
Oh <u>man</u> I gotta get
    out of this place

Fishen' 4 Real Again

Glimmers and gleams
of the themes
or maybe the truth
hints, the only proof
confidence can overcome
hell or wells of death
it's searching each moment
to toss it's fishing line out to drag you down
then you scale the harsh wells
slipping sliding back once in a while
frustration uncontrolled can't make it all
crumble down on you
but you got to make it through to the light at the top
determination strength
to help you go the length
jiving to be living
feeling breathing touching seeing
     Loving
how many times may I have
to free myself from bonds?
maybe I just jump in to be mystified
laugh cry laugh cry
let out a great big sigh
and ask yourself why?
twitch twitch scratch the itch
there were no mosquitoes when I was out of the well
no concerns feeling harmony
cherishing each moment
     spiritually and happily
uplifted by forgiveness
     guided by love

is not only a memory but a goal
to climb myself out of this hole
get less help each time
got to use my own mind
follow your own truth
your own religion
to make beautiful
beautifying not dying
when they talk of death
there is a good chance they are lying
don't know that for sure
you don't wanna hear theories
they just raise too many queries
making me weary
the rain keeps falling
and I may be too
but at least I have a message for you
    some kind of insight or clue
    I wonder who
    will stop the rain
    end the pain
    but me and each of you
cause in the words of Robert Marley
    We don't need no more trouble
let's us pop the bubble...
forgiveness is the work of Love
    thank you Lord

Abandon Ship!

Abandon ship!
    Slaves revolt!
Look down in the deep blue
    it's growing!
This ship ain't gonna support us much longer
    we are burning the hull
        to keep us warm
The man in the look out tower
    forgot to look down
The support's losing integrity
    we're gonna drown!
There's a hole in the ozone engine
    and the captain cries
    just one more moment of glory
    let me take my ship down with me
The slaves manning the oars
    hear rumors that we are lost
        not going anywhere anymore
    no new world to be found
        this frivolous journeys going down
We need support
    and the captain cries
        and shoots the spies
    "traitors" he exclaims
        "I know all of your names!"
And the slaves reply,
    "we had all we needed back there!"
This big ole ship is a goin' down.
    going back to solid ground.
"Abandon ship!"

Walking Through Ashes of the Past

While the sidewalk turns to grass
the force of time rewinds
walking through the ashes of the past

the cycle of the planets comes round at last
solo we ride with universal minds
while the side walk turns to grass

and time seems to turn so fast
revealing reality waves of all kinds
walking through the ashes of the past

the cosmic clock ticking eternity's task
low and behold the future from behind
while the side walk turns to grass

slash and burn then feed with ash
replenish and renew nature's wise old mind
walking through the ashes of the past

The messiah rides upon an ass
the truth he's trying to find
while the side walk turns to grass
walking through the ashes of the past

Possibly Revealing

Those are the four horse men!
Coming down across the moon
scattered interpretations
     of those revelations
I stand on the white powder rocks
     accepting most any possibilities
reading it all in to the paradox
is this the real reality?
mystical night for real
are they coming for me?
The intensity of idea climaxes in my mind
a tear comes to mine eye
if I am to die I am to die
     to be one when my suffering is done
lay back on my car, rocks in my lungs
     fear, the poison of a wild mind.
Does the truth ever come with time?
And maybe I wanted to see them so I did
     in the clouds with grace
too powerful and what would I do?
     Stop, wait, they must know...
Go back in the tent
     that's where I went.

Armageddon Is Coming

News lies
for whose benefit?
I don't watch too much
kind of <u>sick</u> of it...
Cows and chickens
dying from heat
Concert fans getting beat
Oh what a story
I'll put it to song
something about Armageddon
it is hot on planet earth
but I can survive
just to watch this
fast moving time
Lemmings on parade
I'm sitting in the shade
from a tree that love made
dolls and things
Sweaty bugs with wings
But I cannot scream
      about this thing
No sense in causing fear
yet it's been caused in me
saw by the clouds and on the tv
heard in too many a place
"speeding up near the end"
you can't ignore signs flashing in your face
make your self pure my friend
where the tracks lie for the last train to glory
they say less damage
to the ozone
but it's not getting any better

Pure + Natural

Pure + Natural
is my thumb
is my heart?
or is it numb
I can help myself
as long as I don't take too much
I should be giving
not worrying about getting
giving love is not easy
if you don't feel you get what you give.
I want to live
I scream out every day
I scream out
    Father! I feel your breeze
    inside of me
and out around me
    Mother! Why do I feel this pain
I don't belong in pain
not in fear
let me be in this love
I talk about
let me do my job
He who rides with fear is a devil ain't it clear
I want to be free to forgive my brothers
    if I'll be forgiven for this beer
Marching to the fields
    of joy is my job
I will lead you to the fields of joy
when I become more than a boy
I give with the Lord's love
the most wonderful gift from above
hey, before we'll be free
I will march in your love march
I will ride your love train
I will tell my brother to end his pain
              when I figure it out of my brain

Whom Shall I Fear

Whom shall I fear
when my truth is clear
I now must seek
to relieve myself of
    my errors
to confront my fears
    with the truth
coming into this situation
    on my thoughts
not being scared of getting
    caught
I know all that glitters
    is not gold
and from my heart
    truth can be told
letting it be
    with unity
sowing the seeds
    of love
so my fears I may
    rise above
when I don't hide
    I got the vibes
and I feel
    that I am real
amongst the confusion
something shines
    through
and if that's where
I'm looking
it's got to be
    true
I'm ready to listen
    for my next lesson
and I can speak
    although at times

I can feel weak
So I will let be
    all which I cannot
    rightfully
    alter
    and not feel bad
doing my growth
where I am most dying
So when I look around
I can see that I'm really
    flying
resisting passively what
    I should not do
until I don't got that
    desire
rising above the
    fire
    higher
    higher
    vibrations
    of being
not only listening
but acting
on this message
    given to me
so I may be
above the hole
my will unwillingly
    led me to fall into
and I know that the love
    inside of You
is no different
    than that in me
and with a few good
    words
I may learn to.......see

At A Rabbits Pace

Though you seek your union
you may waste your time.
Is it better to speak of meaningless things
or to sit in silence?
Who defines meaninglessness?
How do people come to different beliefs?
As you gaze into the eyes of the nonliving
what do you realize but what you already know?
How do you know that what you understand
      is what people are truly saying.
I then frowned as darkness fell upon me
I then smiled
and the light broke
      and the darkness curled up on its side.
Raise your arms little girl, open them to the light
      and time is not wasted.
To kids everything is serious,
they even play seriously
making sure that everyone knows the rules
but not that they follow them.

I write poems.
What is a poem?
      who defines what is what?
The dictionary says that
      "life is the property or quality manifested in functions such as metabolism, growth, response to stimulation, and reproduction, by which living organisms are distinguished from dead organisms or from inanimate matter."

Life is a property owned by one or
      a quality manifested.
Manifestation - if we have the same definition
      is the creation of something or to put it to action
      as I manifest my wildest dreams.
Though you seek life
you really seek a condition of stimulus.
As the view of the rainbow withdrew,
I closed the window.

Then I opened it to let the light shine in
as the little girl had done many months ago.
I wasn't born yet.
Where are you when you're not born
    living, dead, or inanimate
the place at which everything is true
maybe that's heaven
or in reality...
maybe there is no heaven
But what's after life?
Is there an afterlife?
When we die are we dead?
Where is JFK
    is he in the heart of another kid?
All of the elements were created by particles
and formed on to the earth
    evolution
    revolution
    chaos, destruction
    is that the end?
No tis not.
Thinking of rose petals on an autumn spring day
I may realize what life is.....may not
who developed the english language?
    who? and why?

Last night at another place
I discussed with myself
who owns what?
The Indians didn't believe in property
I was in a sweat lodge once
    sweated my ass off

playing in the street
    like little kids
chasing a cat up a tree
different realities: in the mind of the cat
huge creatures are going to catch me and eat me

in the mind of the children: that cat sure is fast!
What is fast if it can't be compared to something slow?
What is any word if it can not be compared to another?
    the world is filled with opinions
ugh, gross!
nasty
"wow how wonderful" the garbage man said
point of view
point of attachment
for some teenagers its the mouth

trouble makers
breaking signs
    why damage property if it only comes back to you
    with higher prices for food.
What is food?
Necessary to survival.
People have strange reasoning
    what is strange
    but an opinion
something different in everybody
facial expression hinted clues
tinted shoes blue black
    why is that?

The leaf fell languidly from the tree branch
bouncing off of air currents
it landed on the dew covered windshield
of my mother's vehicle.

I took a vacation
with revelation
change the station.
Music is a part of everyone' s life
going to the bathroom is also
what isn't?

If you believe,
    what is true

maybe you are right
I guess,
      no, I know that.
If you believe something,
      it's true in your world.
So MY world
      is better than yours
cause I only believe
      what I want.

What I want
is peace.
I believe in peace.
What is peace
      who has the definition?
Most people say
      peace is the absence of conflict
English language
In order to be defined it is compared to war
that's not a knife! and this is...
there you go all over again as the bird sings
a tune carries to another part of the wood
joy and laughter resign
where destruction once reigned
fat remains undefined without
skinny
reverse
fast forward
stop and play
today
gay? happy or homosexual
no yes
what do you want to hear

I want nothing but to learn
to learn of what
      to learn of magic and light
      darkness and destruction
who cares about you or what will happen

everyone
because if I'm not alive
than neither is anyone else.
That is my perspective
in my world.
I he she him her
what are these for
we should be able to get our point across
with gestures
or thoughts
higher thoughts
lower thoughts
all based on something else.
We speak a codependent language.

Last night at another place
a man came and told me of peer pressure
and how it affected his life
smoked pot, drank a lot
he was a biker
now just a motorcycle enthusiast.
What classifications we put ourselves in

I bet I learn more from my self
writing
than I will learn in one whole year
of public schools
at least a lot more useful stuff
everyone is a teacher
and everyone is a student
right brain left brain let's come together
forge a mighty path
into the never ending
where the sun and the moon collide
and life love and laughter become eternal.
As I once was before I was born
years ago.

So I speak my opinion to others

Who absorb and let pass
Truth is
    they know more about themselves
    than I do
So I speak what I know
    to see what they feel

What do I have to lose?
You would think some people would be more open to you
doesn't hurt to be nice or helpful

Life isn't real or is it
as I asked before
what is real?
As dreams seem more real than life,
    and the clown dances
    thru the streets
thru the streets, where is that?
down up, or all around
something that comes about when we all think of something.

I don't believe in a single souled God
but if you do I'm perfectly happy with that
for what one believes is his choice and his choice alone
yet he should know about everything else
as the bloodred streets that lined the town
lay in destruction life is all over for great great Ed
    but starts again for little Mary.

who is luckier?
what is luck?
    is it good or bad?
I guess that it is good
    unless the word bad
    is in front of it!

Three people were standing in the dessert
    you ruined my pies
do you get it

dessert, desert
without common sense you can't speak and understand
english
british, french
we are all from the same planet, call us
earthlings
or how about Milky Wayans
why discriminate by countries or states or even
      why discriminate by color
that is all that you care about
self interested behavior

as he holds out his hand for the camera
      is he waving or requesting?

meaningless messages sent through the airwaves
sometimes you don't know
      whether dreams are more real than life
maybe they are
as people pass down sidewalks
the world is still turning
the flowers still growing
The world sits on the lamp
      for the lamp
           is the sun.

AND THIS

canto uno

Let there be a beginning with an end
and again
and again
and let it flow
for who's to know
and comprehend
the cosmic forces
but the brain of man
and we grow
evolve
find our own poles
to say
to show some what of what you know
prepare your self with explanations
as if you will be judged
and be and see
and draw in a world of meanings
to nothing
yet something
like the time
and this a message mysterious
yet nothing is strange
while everything is strange
living in false worlds false times
spending false dollars false dimes
all for feelings all for time
questing to make the mystery
a reality
to make the love
a reality
to make sanctity
a reality
and to make freedom
a norm defined
to be one with our problems
to be one with our solutions
to be one with the earth
to be one with man kind

to be one with our planet
and to have a hell of a time doing so
that will make the stories
and a pleasant drama of true love.

Canto Dos

Psychology is misunderstood
the study of the mind
the study of the soul
and what do they think they know
I want the understanding of the capabilities of the mind
to be challenged
enough of letting people limit themselves
concentration
motivation
co - ordination
I want laid back
I want to live in fortresses in the trees
and to p___ off the edge
to nourish the soil
to s___ off the edge
and nourish the soil
to grow food above the trees
closer to the sun
to accept death
to let our dead fall out of the trees
and the animals to feed
to recycle and re-use
harmony...dig it
let everyone be a growing cat
and let them cat until they die
to say it straight and not regret
to accept the wrong and to make it right
so what is wrong
let us not pay taxes
let us do the share to keep us alive
and enjoy
quality time
I want a peaceful realization revolution!

Let us confront the problems
and overcome without regret
just laughter
to not get caught by trivial
misguided actions
laugh and overcome
understand the truths of our tongues
the polarities of heaven and hell
and the power of the family
of the mind
let us show no fear
and all be our own heroes
let it be good to be good
and not good to be bad...
who's to say what is good or bad
I say let it be in flow
and let it roll
cause progression is not progress
anymore anyhow
we are all Jesus
and our earth is heaven/purgatory/or hell
what do we want to progress to
or does anyone care anymore...
I do am I innocent or guilty?
good or bad?
depends on the eyes you catch me with
as many worlds as there are minds
the good rubs off
the bad is rubbed in
and I say let it rub off
be you, honestly
and the good is same as bad
all of the polarities
are all the same
they are all just happening
grasp the ungraspable
and go beyond that
ask a question to yourself
then the question beyond that
beyond that

find all of the answers
speak of your honest answers
and compare
and relate
think for every one
think for yourself
and the key work is think
let us go beyond
conditioned response
into situation response
conscious response
observe the mistakes of the bugs
relate
observe the achievements of the bugs
relate
people, animals, bugs = scenery
the environment
a text book
observations
past realizations
and your mind the most evident
scenery
yet so mysterious
let loose
let go
let flow...
dig the innocent love
as I honor a tree
it has time and will to listen
it can't run away
from truth
it only lives as a vibe
as we do
-let it hit you-
and feel it, dig it
don't scare from words
scare not by anything
its all just a phase
and a difficult maze
symbolize and relate...

On the Train

To relax a while, while I ride this train
looking at who's going home again
look around getting comfortable
pushing bags that get in their way
she pushed it back after her
      nervous day
wind can blow up the skirt
      she wears
just to show her panty hose tears
make a face just to get a laugh
from a man walking on his repetitious path
all dressed the same
they try not to show their pain
but you get the good and you get the bad
really it's TIME that we wish we had
riding these trains going to and fro
always moving always on the go
I won't end up like the rest
trying to find a way out of this mess
why was I born, it seems they say
"I didn't know it would be this way"
worn and tired tired and worn
made to get up every morn
this is business........this is work
standing waiting at the door
who am I working for?
"they give me money but I need more
I got a house it's not too big
never see it, never did
but I pay its tax and I pay my bills
I'll just leave it in my will
forgotten how to have fun
go to sleep when my work is done"
Saturday night they have some drinks
so they won't have to think
saving for vacation time
not wanting to lose their minds
noticing what they have to lose
their time flying, it's on the loose

Simple 1

Walk in laugh in
Smile turn around
    rub nose
almost lose balance
    on heel
hands in pockets
eyes in sockets
    in air
buy drink by the pound
    beans by the sound
    follow, you ready
TV volume off - mute
Radio is on - tune
Both on - time
play same beat
    and same beat
audio visual sink
ironies and tea
is that good its good
pretty good that's pretty
    they was talking for a long time
didn't say much
just pretty good.

Simple 2

In sights to a simple mind
or just un aware or
    with out care
and they long for friends
    talk attention!
I have coffee
    I'm nice sad
unhealthy spit and twitch
    and still shake to breathe
Stare and think I shouldn't
    snap out of it
just don't have the happy head bob
    for apples and oranges
still have something in common
go rotten, if not devoured
good not plot every hour
want to see what'll play tonight
    remember that movie?
when I tripped on
my thoughts I was Art
You art art miss take
    another picture
for my new born frame
lady dressed in black
tripped on a little crack, did not
look back twitch in mine
odd pulse stroke like
a strobe light
tried to drink with cap half
way on cream soda
all over my chin
head for sat turn
    left a round brim
    round head
I slide through the doors as
they open for me....call it luck
good timing by God
    by me
those good days.

Tune Jazz

Stay tuned in all day...
    where ever you go!
tuned in to
    the universal vibe
    or the tone of the tune in your room
your own tune
    can't weep
broom, for the dirt
shirt.
    spilled a little squirt
timid
people try to hold laughs in
    or look at the sadder side
as it is funny and sad
    allusion, to the bad
            get up, cause havoc
    it's all weird
            heads turn
    hands over mouths
            straw slurping
    never ending
            suck
    please don't please do
look hard in the sea
    through the
rampage game-
-boat on a ballet note
No Smo! Mo More!
king was smo
the rain, the people
the city, babble on
kids don't see me in line
wanderin in on a mission
out of line?
In spite of my ration
man, you are
on my nerve us.a.break down
government   I'll break it down
go veare men "tah

veare um for us
make them a bide law
to shape the tide
as the moon reflects.

The Choice of Our Head

Now and again refrain
 from ghastly dips and dooze
In spirit in flesh a touch of pain
 the price of our dues
Now and again comes the rain
 responding to the paths we choose
In life, maybe in death
 it is love sought to keep and not to lose
A choice awaits with every breath
 to think what I will, surrender to the news
Each revelation another step
 try not to slide back into the blues
to think of times we slipped and why we wept
 to worry or be happy we may simply choose
Fear of hell or desire for paradise
 entangle us in the web
 only our inner selves to lose
by revelations deep within let us be led
 as on the idea of love we muse
to discover the cause for which we bled
 true knowledge shall not be abused
With this love if we are amply fed
 to reside in unity as we choose
This can all be thought of,
 as we lay ourselves to bed.

Blow Your Mind Automation

Merchandising is never spasmodic
blossom dish click events
flick special, Tonight!
    far-flung but thoughtful
clean disintegration chamber
give recognition to entropy
      entirety of the paradox
step by step to debase the
black mailer of syncronicity

crone on the delicious parade
    in the mirror
adult entertainment industry
calypso abbreviations of the
      Classical Hollywood cinema
on the jam of toast of all toast!

Gothic clock of exfoliation
no ordinary time
The arsonist sage is burning
    the divine comedy.

Spy the great American spectator
  with an unquiet mind full of blah imagery
Synonyms of the X-phone
and the English language retail of
the psychosomatic how to howl like Ginsberg
    buff it up with southern humor
vintage pictures of youth forgotten
and an unadulterated freak of reality dance
timeless in its essence yet so shatterable
to be smashed like a thousand dollar wine bottle
some how placed in a bar fight
inexplicable but not misplaced
    and it all seems to swirl back
so mysteriously

seen only at the time of chaotic harmony
when you once flowed with the seas of change
unknowing the wills of the strange
happy go lucky...
To become as a child once more
visualizing perspective reality
and the frugal ties of desiring eyes
no attachment little discernment
of the eve and dawn.
Yeah there are those who could tell you it all
on a good day...
By The WAY.

It Is Or It Isn't

Laid back in a half circle chair
looking at the castle in my cigarette ash
pain is a sensation as every thing else
my shirt lights up burning, look to see
I was off on a space dream
twirling in and out of the now
stretching the chaos within
tree like thoughts branching off
from the same trunk
it only seems to be chaotic
rolling through purposes
it runs smoothly automatic
looking back in time
supposing instances never to happen
only to be thoughts in my mind
the kangaroo pouch of ideas
where they seem to float in from nonexistence
striking into the now
I feel and interpret it how I choose
in this machine in Gods mind
smoothly oiled to operate the possibilities
for junior to wash his hands for dinner
punctuality running its course
for mom to prepare for the American Dream
as I sit on the outskirts of their reality
to stretch it's realm as it all must expand
and confusion sets in as I free wheel
around the deterministic man
no one need to know all
everything that is now predicts
what is to be a second from now
except he who knows where
 my eye may chance to fall
this is the chaos of it all
what makes me see one word
over another
like the birds of a feather
my how this tends to be like that

all interconnected by the cycles and cranks
clockwork universe one story reality
who has to see the second floor
or step down stairs to the below ground lairs
I once told my self it is or it isn't
can it not be both. Expecting the unexpected.
I roll through this vision of confusion
between extremes goodness lies
I roam without limitation
my mind opening the ties
nomads of the now to well round
restyle to the times transgression
glide in the haze as the castle burns down
the boys at the firm are having a field day
the clocks escapement lets another minute slip away
as I come back to extinguish the flame
burning done, no time to distinguish blame
and so is erratic chaotic?
Or purposely placed as a counter weight
no real hierarchy may exist
how may one be higher without
one just as important being lower
and they just are.
Material worth a hill of beans
eschatology auctioned by all means
as in my silence I see the film flicker in the night
true representation of liquid destiny
following each incarnated identity
Where shines the light of Mitrha?
Reflecting a kaleidoscope of realities
in each mind as it all seems true
as it is or it isn't must each of us
intuitively comprehend
truths mystically unproven by others
as we see it
So be it.

The Sanctuary Cutter

The sanctuary cutter
    so, sigh, ahh tea
driving force
going nowhere fast
    faster...
Time expiring
    ever so tiring
wild horses in process
    domestication
with the occasional futile
    vacation
more luxury less scenery
dessert harvesting
    spree
sanctuary cutters
and criminal factories
    so sigh ahh Tea
want more good ole stuff
    my american journey
what ever happened to
    the climbing of trees
children of self interested
    control dramas
over protectivity
what's rising up
    surprising
the plague
    crowds
    and power

hand in hand
or hand on head
because, my friend they
treat their kids
as society treats them
a temptress
    that says no
Like they, just say
you just say yes
    then ask for ice water
you get just ice
tragic magic
things fall apart
there's a need to recognize
the departure of the divine
    ugly ways
make ugly waves
there is a rising tide
    bubbling identities
around the world
    boiling in a tea pot
ready to let out a ear
piercing
    scream
to let off some
    steam
to sit once again in zen
    citizen of the
    world

Emotional Propaganda

Desiring the unreal
predressing what is to come
and forgetting the possibilities
this is to be subtitled self fulfilled prophecy
manifesting the foreseen destiny
there is a ultimatum possibility
dinosaurs speak to the radioactive
bombshelters to prolong suffering
why live in atomic catastrophe
yeah I want to feel too
more unfilling hype I want to
soak in the subliminal epitome
of sexual flashes of fantasy
true romance seems too good so scary
what is delightfully dirty...
A fools game where one looks down in shame
this dirty world reflects into our souls
fake masks are worn as the truth is torn
real love forgotten passed off as fantasy
real meaning has meandered to the bottom of the sea
the boys sit in the barroom and smile
the old boys lounge their being all the while
eyes show a dimming light of hope
greet a stranger as you would God
more than a glance and a nod.
What of real love.

My Will Doesn't Own

Casually oriented for ever green
   winter days
unchaining the bonds of frustration to lean
   on yesterways
of coping and dealing you new hands
   to play
and up walks Will, who as he lands
      says enchante`
      I don't have to worry...
      I don't think...
Unfilled of self thought and in his
charge it's a flick of the wrist
for a pencil to fall, for an igloo
incense burner to light and be set aglow
I don't say my, chappy, I don't say
   my at all
Casually oriented for paisley leaves
   of the fall
the discussion of what we don't know
ensues ensures no
conclusion yet opts a smile
I don't have to worry...
      I don't think...
And who ever put the quarter in the
   juke box.
As it plays, whoever's pick
it's a dwindling of chapstick
you can hear Will say "don't say
my at all" and the television roars.
And "why be may be material girl
Shudder I to the real" as the channel
flipping stops on a fishing show
   as if you didn't know
Will doesn't think he has to worry
and he doesn't have to worry because
   he doesn't think
and the next song played who ever

didn't pick who knows. Every
thing is possessed
I don't say my at all
to grasp the fish by the jaw
to pull it out of the water
casually oriented Will kept cool
I don't have to worry
        I don't think

This is the Nineties...

Like a funky chair in the sped up past
this is the 90's yeah well, this is now and I exist as well
and it just can't be too much more boring
Nobody seems to talk of life
just of fear
complaining 'bout work and those they
think are no good, talking 'bout the end of the world
and were all gonna die someday
don't think you have something to do...
throwing out the old just to be new.
Spend time walking in your green and tan style
eyes missing the fact all the while
looking like you are looking
or you don't care any more
Forsaken the trees for the Babylonian whore
and your blues ain't like mine.
Rather cynical I know least it only attack values
mingling through the halls of lives
to find something to take your mind away
These people, kind and strong
need something to make them get along
we need a dragon to slay...
why don't we all agree on one
O' such different intricate characters
shifting through in and out of my view
I wonder if they know
     how they learn...
I hope we all don't give up hope.

Out Side

There are no judgments but your own
you are the only thing you own
looking for your home
so, do you know where you come from?
and, why you ventured out?
did you find what you sought?
hope you don't get caught.
there's a soul in the woods
whose side is he on?
do you see him at night?
Is he gone by the dawn?
do you serve some one some thing some cause?
do you feel some presence
when your whole worlds at a pause
is it fear or love?
who does this to you?
just keep on walking
      with faith you'll make it through
and shouldn't it be ok...
      shouldn't it be good?

Rerunning Frantically

Cigarette stuck to his upper lip
in the middle of a cobble stone strip
    with icy snow in the cracks.
His eyes the only thing moving in the street
other than his fingers snapping to an unknown beat
City sounds in the background and devious laughs in the bars around
his mind running on an inexact premonition
where in the best of his words
devils and angels, a heavenly vision
these people had glares uncanny
    of love and purity
and he does not want to judge
rerunning frantically
Was I talking to them?
were they talking to me?
he wasn't there in the streets...
busily pondering...
              his mind wandering...
scared by a thought
A devil.   good God!
smoke ran circles around his hat
    I could not bear the thought
some power, yes some power,
    and those laughs,
        at him?
and so he laughs at them...
    to not be afraid
what can anyone do?
Steal your soul?
    heavens no...
BRIGHT LIGHTS! Hey pal keep on walking!
    Get out of the way!
so he walked on and wondered if he <u>was</u> in the <u>way</u>.
All the pieces fit together
                too well.
who is the puzzler who's hand fastens them so wittily,
and who was he to be in it and so
becoming part of it.
sitting down

        sewer grates a steaming.
and the cold air plays with his eyes
      swirling on the bricks behind.
      like the intellect in his mind.
"I want to be a good guy"
 while those laughs they grow stronger.
for that moment, not much longer.
    and he laughs back.
got a light?
      tattered and torn.
man asks for a light
     luminescence for his being
-a flash thought- this is a chance
light is all around us what you seek is flame...
and why would you seek flame?
     for the pleasure and pain.
Simple could be a cure, and the man said,
"I've already given up
       give me a flame'
what a shame? and so he had one too
"I'll figure it out tomorrow."

Where We Have Been

Strewn in the toss of eyes and laughs
spun like a top unwhirled
in unfeeling self absorbed arms
I attempt to rest

Speak child speak let me
know what you know
let me see where you've been

connect to something and focus
all your force in ways unknown
to tell me where you've been
to show me how you've grown

"Where's that twinkle in your eye
 that shows you care?" And his reply,
"In this dark forest of stress and denial
I try to strike a match through the purple leaves
 dangling from the branches
of the craggy twisted trees
 their trunks swirling in unsure cranks
the insane cores hollowed out by
 over procreative termites
also unsure of any direction
 as I wander in a time eclipsed by troubles
and the solutions have six swords fending off results
 you ask for a twinkle
when the wind blows out my match before it's lit.
        To roll to roll to roll
 and do you see my point
                        or stab against? For you know
        it's not the wind that has put you here
it's not the stars nor the rain
        which cause your pain
in the deepest channels of your heart left untouched
        a cool breeze blows. A river flows
and reflects what hopefully is to be

A twinkle. A light! Trunks thicker than before
when strangers are no longer strangers anymore
when there are no walls... Only open doors.
then my eye will twinkle like never before
the fires will light ever more bright
and I will ask you where you've been..."

Visionary

Will someone give me that universal dictionary
I don't want my words to be fictionary
what I want to know is if the muffin
will jiggle on my food tray today
I strain this radical cling free movie
tie not for death will do part
yet love possibly an immortal tie
see the indefinite discourse
of the eye figment energy
to discredit the industry for selling our souls
for who was it who bought our demise
the devil in us sells ourselves short
the true square dance of commerce
My ship becomes numb degaussed
unattracted to excessive frivolities
only owning you forsaking Joys for toys
there is a massive degeneration of beauty
cause you can't see what's not embodied
what are you serving and who are you protecting
when you take away my fun?
Friskiness rolls in the forest of my mind
merry chauffeur of joy
I reel back in time
to see this worlds decline
I visioned the twirling dance of love
all of us with a common blood
I visioned the colors of joy
hearts and souls one dance of innocence
some goal better than material
let go I ask for a day
could you dream this with me and Dr. King?
could you imagine with Lennon?
could you strive with Ghandi?
could you love with Jesus?
could you be loved?
God only knows
I'm a goin to chant down Babylon!
Armageddon grant righteousness!
to be loved by one and all to love one and all

Heart and Soul

I once sat by the sliding glass door on a dark stormy night
decided God did not exist and questioned how space was limitless
still very young I asked God to prove his existence, crying for a light
I wanted my questions answered I hoped that they were heard
and so down the road I learned to see the mysteries of reality
I learned to see all of you as God teaching me

There is a place called home some call it Heaven
we are to realize our unity by loving unconditionally
I have a deep rooted desire to make this life worth living
I feel it is now our roll to relinquish our control
to return this world to God's hands
let us forsake the devil's play land

I know that nothing you can buy will bring you ultimate happiness
your perception forms your idea of reality so question the possibilities
sometimes you got to let loose into the flow in order to feel bliss
live in the moment without care for tomorrow's affairs
walk in the proud land and have a sense of shame
don't get too caught up in attention stealing games

Be sure to seek and speak the truth with no fear with no regret
speak for your self don't force feed what you think is wealth
listen to the wind speak of good and bad
      through the barbershop quartet
you are justified to say what you feel and to eat
      your share of every meal
you can not run from yourself don't seek reasons to escape
don't forsake the dirty dog for God comes in every shape

Keep integrity in your character through night and day
positive and negative are in perspective
and though I've stumbled many a time I'm still on my way
keep a good head in the darkest hour
do you want bliss or do you want power?
the world is a temple and requires respect and care
you have a destination then you are half way there.

An Essay on What Needs to be Said

Reality is not in perspective all of the time. Sometimes all of reality is in perspective. For some people reality is never in perspective. Some say reality is always in perspective. Maybe slices of reality are in perspective until you get a pie in the face. The definition of reality is like any other definition so you would have to interpret it as you will depending on what you believe the definitions of the individual words mean. Define this then define all of the words you used to define the first and so on and on shall I say et cetera. Perspective is just another word. Words get boring and frustrating and seldom mean all that much. They only mean something when whoever is reading them does not have anything else on their mind. I don't dislike words, just their unused potential and their misused capabilities. The confusing relationships of those who think they know what is being talked about when they don't. But, who am I to knock on anything in this world? I could do the same. How do you take complements? I respond to criticism much better. Someone give me another slice of reality pie. If you hit me in the face try to miss my eye. Any way you want it, that's the way you get it, any way you want it! But anyway for the time, being is good, I feel, and that is my definition of real for the time being. B is a letter in the alphabet.

A Haiku

Jack frivolousy rat
in a cage
for decoration

Butterflies and Bees

When a butterfly
    lands on my nose
I can feel its love
    don't worry 'bout which way it goes
but if it were a bee
    I wouldn't want it near me
if I were scared of its sting
where it would fly to I would want to see
Making me afraid of the bite
    or the possibility thereof
wanting to see the beauty
    and feel a butterfly's love
If a country has a bomb
    we might smack it out of fear
If a bee has a stinger
    would you let it linger
    or land on your finger
when swatting a bee
    if you miss it'll just get miffed
I'd rather be a butterfly
    and why don't you ask me why
Love is the ultimate weapon
    of the truth
look into my eyes on that one
    for your proof

I Want to Break Society's Toys

I want to break society's toys
I don't want to break their respect
I want to smash things
But don't want people to pay for it.
I want to mess things up
But want to make them right
I want money but, lose time
I want time but have no money
When will I have time to
      BE HERE NOW
I want to teach
But not mislead
I want to help
they think I'm mad
united we stand
divided we fall
                    we fall
                                We fall
"is there anybody out there???"

Defunkatizer

I saw a new fangled people
        defunkatizer
in the back of a truck
        a man sitting there
with his hand to hold it up
I guess they made it for a grade
but it defunked their style
        just being around it
        for awhile
they took it to the military
another tool to control
another defunker of soul
but, I couldn't stop it
don't know if I should try
if my funk gets taken down
I might as well die
Unless they would build a new
        machine that would funkafie me
        back to who I should be
        Funky.

In the Fog, No, Out of It

Car are far dar bar
do you know who I are
everlasting depended thought
It tried to escape but the snake got caught
perplexed how did it wander
confused did the poor snake ponder
the ways of the trial, the ways of the walk
the feeling it got when it was caught
it had wandered too far or was it too near
it went down by that dock over by that pier
poor guy bundled up with trembling fear
poor guy didn't know the snake was there
but he caught the snake
a frog on the lake
a cookie little sitting in here
we all want that cookie
      we all want that beer
he wants a cigarette to hold in his hand
the snake will travel throughout the land
Mountains of oceans of water and birds
finally someone gets what it's for
but unfortunately that someone is no more
cause the poor guy didn't mind being poor
he ate that snake and licked that frog
after it was over he left in the fog

Twisted Wire

If you don't accept what pain you feel
how will you know if it is real
if you don't accept the pain
you forget how to accept the good
or do you know, and if you could
straight into your fools friends fun
as I approach and push away your gun.
You can do any of them that you wish
a peach tree swimming in a quarter-sized dish,
the twisted wire of evil intent,
I pushed it one way and it bent,
I told it to go and it went.
I did an experiment once with a rat
gave it a nice home without a cat
but it wasn't happy at all with that
It wanted danger, I desired suspense
I saw the sign and I jumped the fence
I did it to feel like I feel right now
jumped into the muck can't find a towel
you see, I've found, I've done it now
as I walked home I found a pack
smoked em all so I could relax
put a snow blade on that tractor
it didn't work was that rat a factor
I was upset, fled through the back door
don't want to see your face no more...

Soul Less

And you think of it another time
we got to get it all together
peering thru the doors of my mind
don't you know of your perspective
endless dreams of the hourglass
something strange your eyes aren't reflective
soul less creature of desperation
toiling infinitely without recreation
sitting in the back seat with flashing lights
something has happened something not right
now I wander through the forest of thoughts
looking to my left I see you are caught
looking to my left you fell in a pit
You are gone and there I sit
there I sit in meditation
there I sit in contemplation
yelling and kicking
I want to be free
open my eyes
for I cannot see

Picketing and Protesting

Picketing and protesting
all of the ignorance infesting,
our minds worrying about making it on time.
Getting bored of hearing those crimes
that have not changed,
except for the names,
from buy a slave
to rent a slave.
Always worrying about getting paid.
letting the wisdom pass through one ear
and out the other.
We need to get it out of our mouths
and into our brother's
ear if he will hear.
And if you got a message give it to him clear
Wake up and look in the mirror.
Discover why we are here.
We don't need to complain about our scrapes,
or to wear the prettiest capes,
just to be all we are,
and speak our truths near or far.
Letting our inner guides do the judging.
The truth will be the truth,
without budging

Professing and
Addressing
I and I

Politics

Politics Politics
involved in the mess
for all of it is spiritual
and we should pay attention
    to politics
but I'd pay more attention to a blade of grass
at least there I know where I stand
or do I?
I can have better ideas
    in my own place
in my own space
    if I own it
anyway I can deal with my dealings
    and decide my fate
and choose my dates
    or let them choose me
I have to choose my next footprint
I choose where to step
    the next step
I can't let others tell me where
    to step all of the time
why else would God give me a mind
cause your head is there to move you around
    madness yes it is here
    in the world
but let's break down the word
    and see who is mad at who...
        and why
madness only resides
    in those who are mad
but I am satisfied
    blessed and thankful

When You Got Love

When your vision is clear
and the beauty is near
all which you fear
      is illusion
sometimes the ugliest scene
becomes the most beautiful
as a cocoon to a butterfly
when you got love
you can rise above
flying high riding high
when it's in your heart
so is God
and so is Jah
and I and I
and anything on this
beautiful scene
you are not misdirected
you're going right
you don't need to fight

Return of the Undone

It's the return of the undone
chill in the air cause,
    that time you didn't care
it's creepy and crawly
    climbing back
        responsibility
you better respond
    this time
It's the return of the undone
the matter not over
the water unsettled
here comes the wave
like a tidal from the oceans grave
    the issue at hand
from the once forgotten land
    the return of the undone
    Vengeance of the ignored
because you made it bored
trying to float away
on your little ship
it catches up today
coming up on your flank
you better face it or walk the plank.

Corn on the Cob

I tried to tell you
    but you just wouldn't hear
I tried to reach you
    but you just weren't there
can't go all my days
    trying to make you hear what I say
cause I could always try another way...
Hope you learn you lessons
    the best way you can
if they knock you on your head
    I hope you'll understand
I could keep trying to teach you the way it is
but, maybe I have to learn it's none of my biz.
If I just do my best
    to be like I know how
if my actions were my words
    I'd teach you all the while
some times I get to thinking
    that it's not my job
to tell you how to eat
    your corn on the cob.

Your Message

And on my exit
    this message I will leave
you are a walking advertisement
for all you believe.
Through this method
    our thoughts are weaved
from my heart to yours
opening up closed doors
to let the love in
    forever more.
people give me your message
as clear as I give mine
step right up to my picture box
transient transparent
that's my mentality
it's all just a step
    or two or three or four
just a step for the picture to unfold
    to reveal its core
consciousness shift
    whole picture in store
we are all looking from different
    perspectives for the same thing
all looking for the truth
why...
it will set us free!!!

Do you remember what beauty was?

We are in a time of hardships caused by disrespect of the earth and disrespect of our brothers and sisters. Our greatest problem is that we are willing to destroy ourselves and we seem to be doing a good job at it. The news offers us disaster after disaster. The weather is out of balance. We have become victims of the joke of "progress". The punchlines are nothing to laugh at. I feel we have to spread about a new understanding, a peaceful realization revolution, to help us return to the light of life that we have put on the back burner for generations on down the road. We could call that progress. It's time to wake up and abandon our present machine. We need to stop polluting the garden before it's too late. Let us discover the power within, while I ask you once again, do you remember what beauty was?

Nick Wassmer